Mini MUSIC
ALTO CLEF

Songs written by:

____
(YOUR NAME HERE!)

Created By: Zachary Seckman
Catalog: KDP-MBAC-PC
ZSMUSIC PUBLISHING
music made just for you

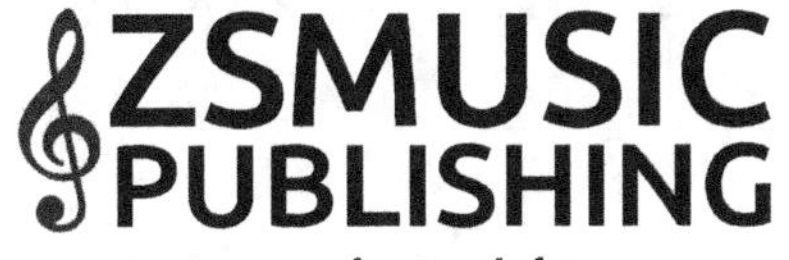

Through the MINI MUSIC books, students are introduced to various concepts through composition. In the Alto Clef Book, students write 36 short songs through given sets of notes on the Alto Clef Staff which leads up to learning 5-note scales of C and G Major, and D Minor. This book is set up for students to write out notes in 4 measures using 4/4 and 3/4 times. The final two songs are blank 8 measure songs for students to write "longer" pieces.

There is also a good mix of titled and untitled songs. Most songs give students prompts to give them inspiration before writing, and some include a blank title for students to come up with their own. Creativity is the goal here, and students should enjoy the composing process. This book gives students a chance to do so, in small chunks so you can fit them in lessons!

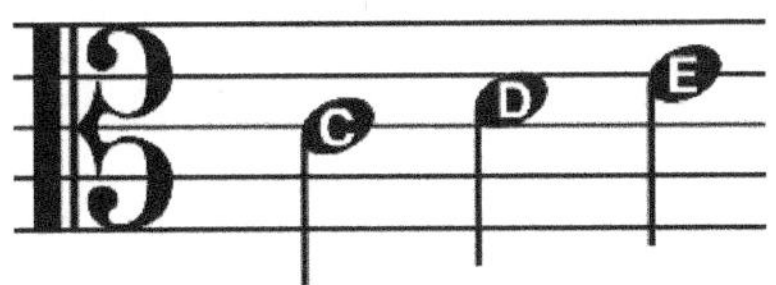

In this part of the book, we will use the C-D-E notes. Write a song by adding one more Quarter Note in each measure below. When you're done try playing your song to see how it sounds! To finish, title your song!

TITLE: ____

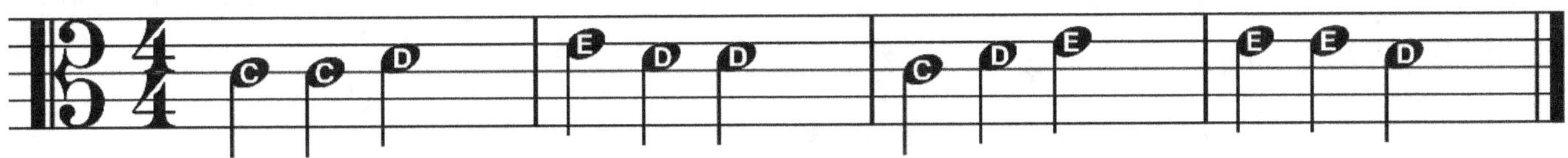

TITLE: <u>CAN DO EVERYTHING!</u>

Do you know someone who can do EVERYTHING? Fill in the measures with two more quarter notes using the C-D-E notes.

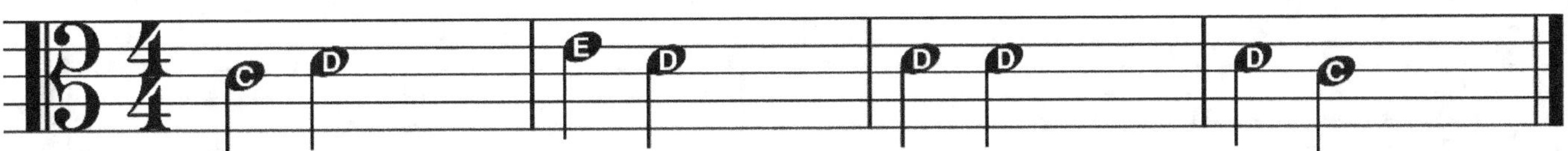

TITLE: <u>HIGHS AND LOWS</u>

Give each measure one more quarter note using the notes C-D-E.

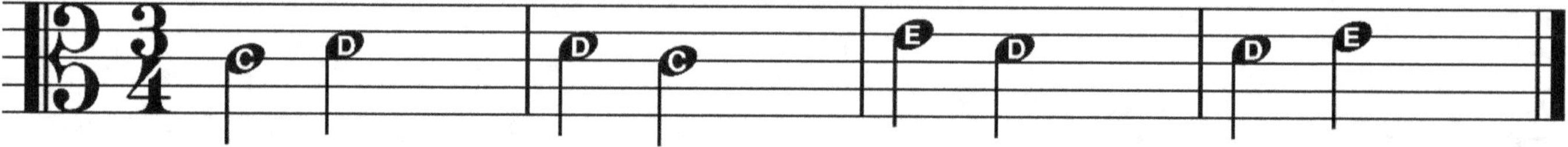

TITLE: <u>IN A SWING</u>

Have you ever had a lazy day that makes you want to go swinging? Using the C-D-E notes, give each measure three more quarter notes to make this song sound like you're in a hammock.

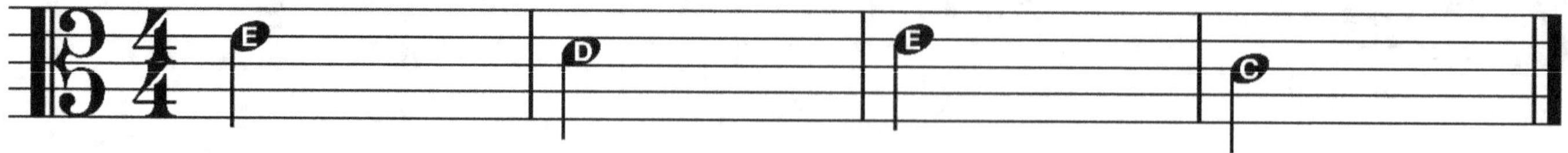

TITLE: ___________________________________

Do you like to go for walks? Have you ever walked up and down hills? Write this song like you're just walking around using the notes C-D-E. Fill in the blank measures below with four quarter notes, then title your song.

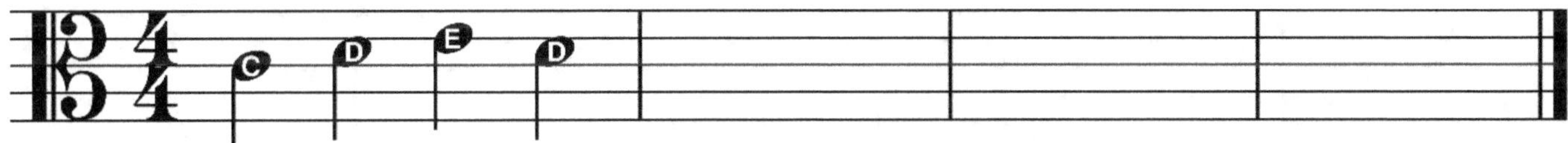

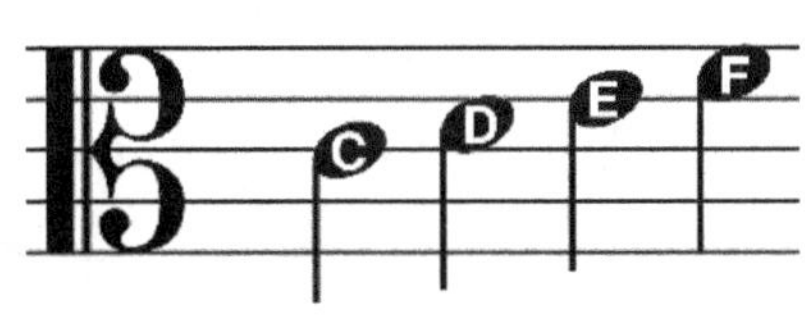

In this part of the book, we will use the C-D-E-F notes. Write a song by adding one more Quarter Note in each measure below. When you're done try playing your song to see how it sounds! To finish, title your song!

TITLE: ___________________________________

TITLE: ____

Complete this song with the notes C-D-E-F by filling in the measure with two more quarter notes. Remember to give this song a title!

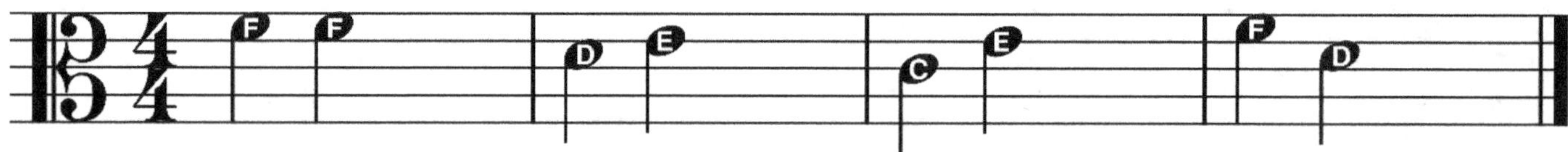

TITLE: <u>GROWING UP</u>

Do you see what the notes are doing? They're moving up the staff! With the notes C-D-E-F, give each measure one more quarter note to finish the song!

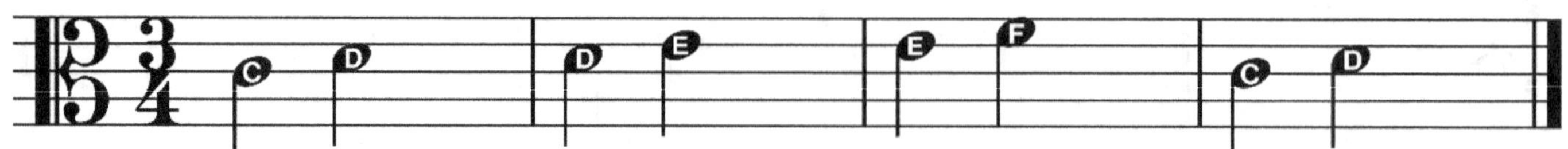

TITLE: <u>DRIFTING DOWN</u>

Think of what happens in autumn when the leaves fall of the trees. With the notes C-D-E-F, come up with a song that is like the leaves drifting down. Each measure needs three more quarter notes.

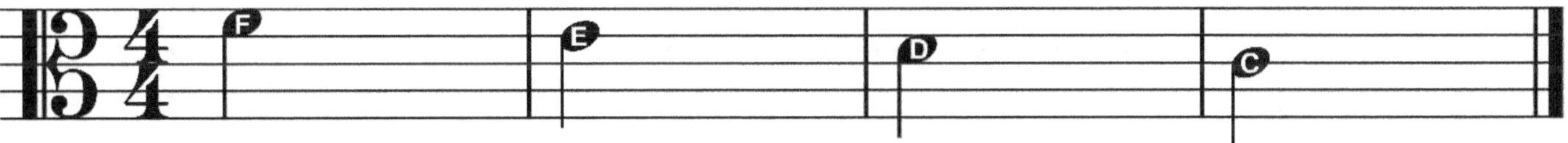

TITLE: <u>WARMING UP</u>

After Autumn, comes winter! Think of a song that would sound "warm" with the notes C-D-E-F and fill in the blank measures with 4 quarter notes.

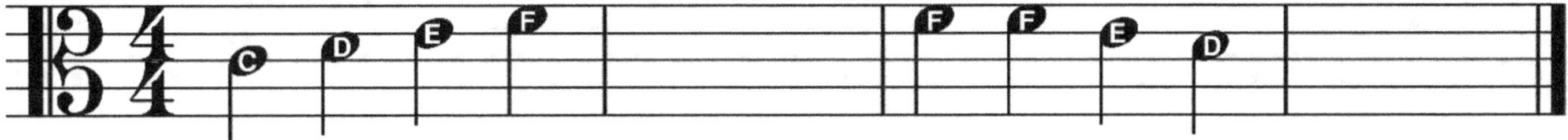

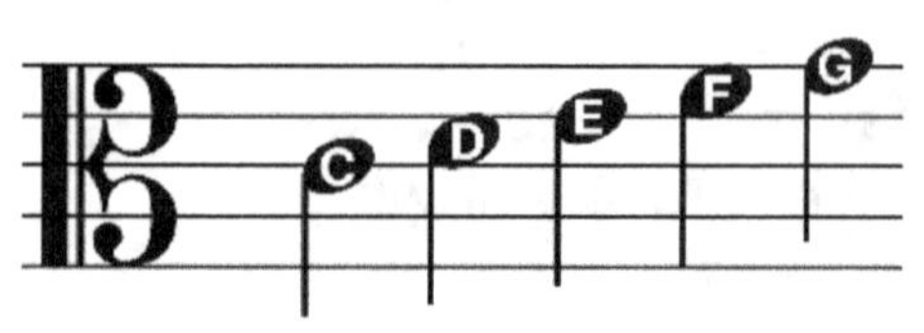

In this part of the book, we will use the C-D-E-F-G notes. Write a song by adding one more Quarter Note in each measure below. When you're done try playing your song to see how it sounds! To finish, title your song!

TITLE: ____

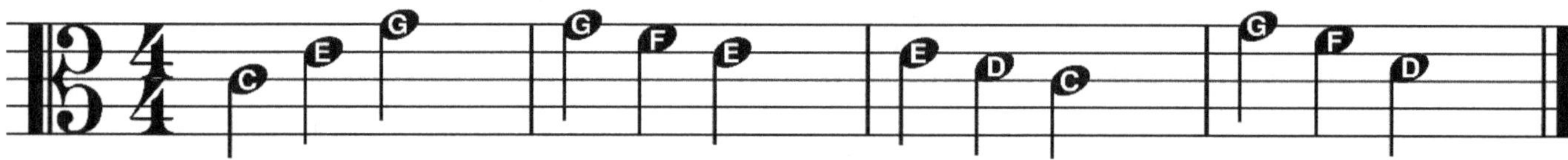

TITLE: <u>GOING DOWN</u>

Still using C-D-E-F-G, come up with a song that would make you think of hills, that go down steeply. Fill in each measure with two more quarter notes.

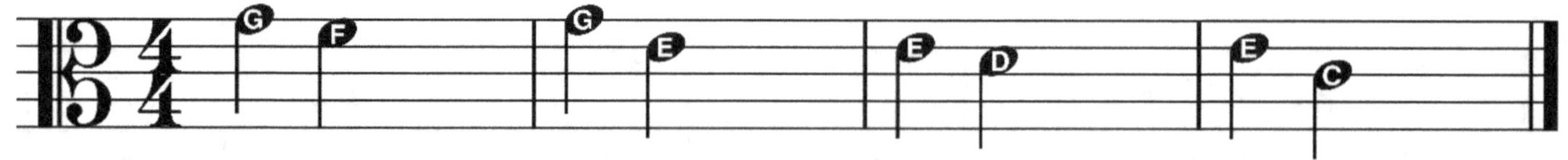

TITLE: <u>A SHORT RIDE</u>

Something that cures boredom is to ride a bike or scooter down the street!
Using the notes C-D-E-F-G, fill in the measures with two more quarter notes!

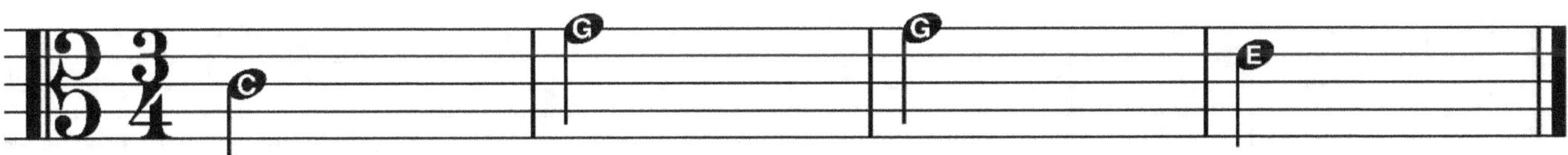

TITLE: ____

While you're riding your scooter, you can feel the wind pushing you as you ride.
How does this make you feel? Use the notes C-D-E-F-G and fill in each measure
with three more quarter notes.

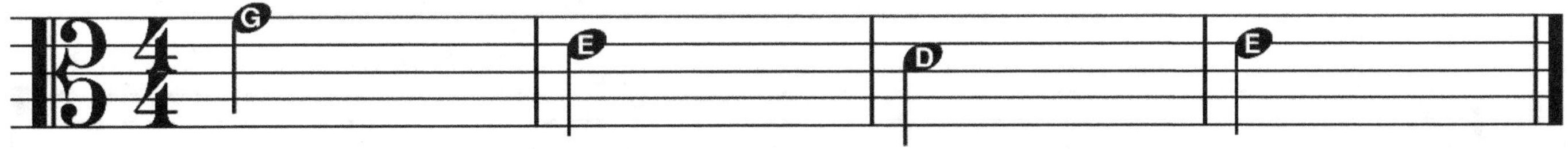

TITLE: _______________________________________

Write a fun song with C-D-E-F-G and title it! Remember that the empty measures need to have four quarter notes in them!

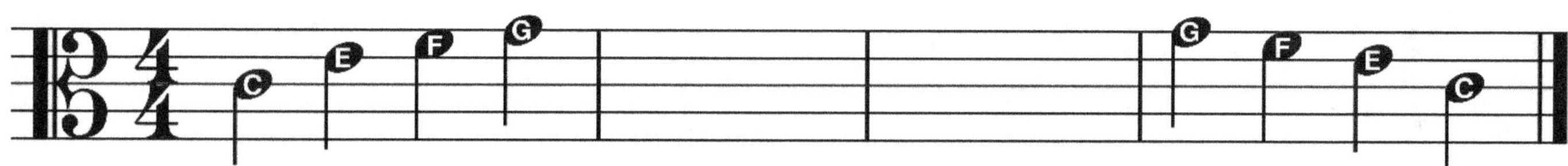

TITLE: <u>A COLD BEVERAGE</u>

It's so hot outside! You need to cool down with something iced and cold! What feeling do you get from the beverage? Using C-D-E-F-G, write a whole song on your own thinking of that drink! Each measure needs four quarter notes.

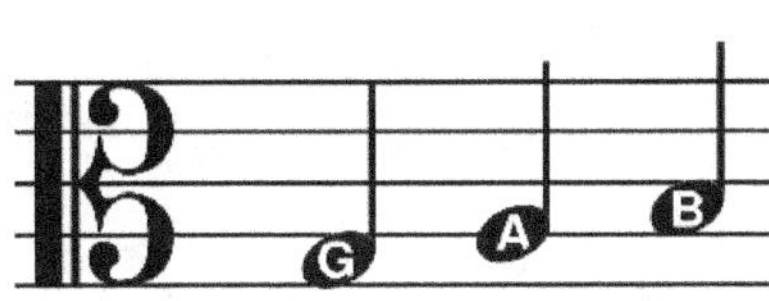

In this part of the book, we will use the G-A-B notes. Write a song by adding two more Quarter Notes in each measure below. When you're done try playing your song to see how it sounds! To finish, title your song!

TITLE: ____

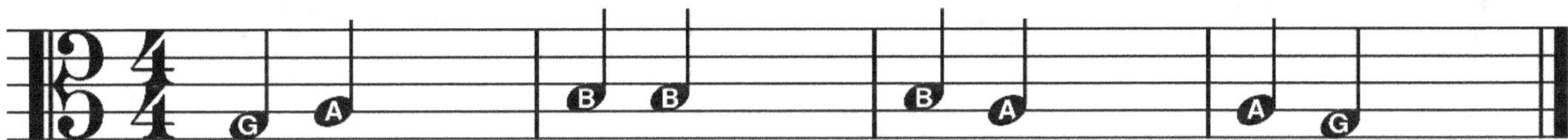

TITLE: <u>MY NEW BIKE</u>

Walking in the park isn't quite fast enough for you, so you want a bike to move about. Using the G-A-B notes, write a Biking Song. You should add three more quarter notes to each measure to finish the song.

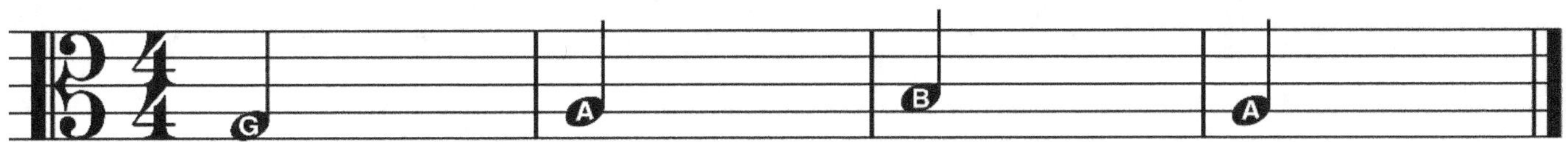

TITLE: ____

Finish out this G-A-B song with two more quarter notes in each measure, and then title your song!

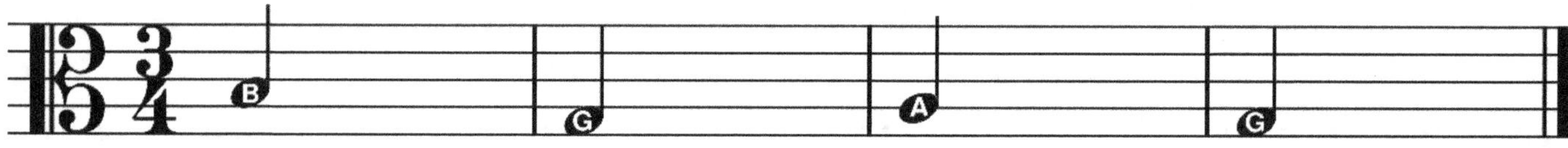

TITLE: <u>WATCHING E-SPORTS</u>

The big e-sports tournament is coming up and you're excited for it! Write out this song thinking of the games coming up by filling in the blank measures with four quarter notes of G-A-B.

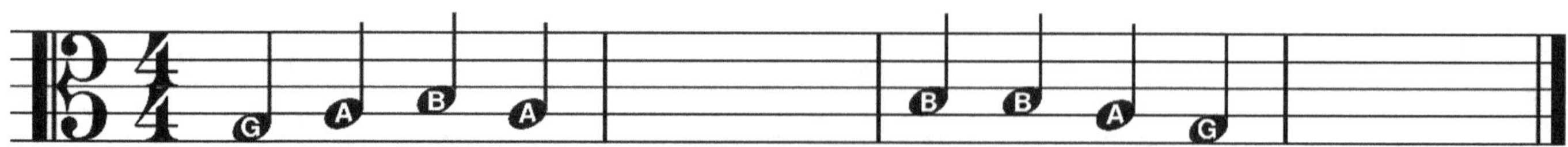

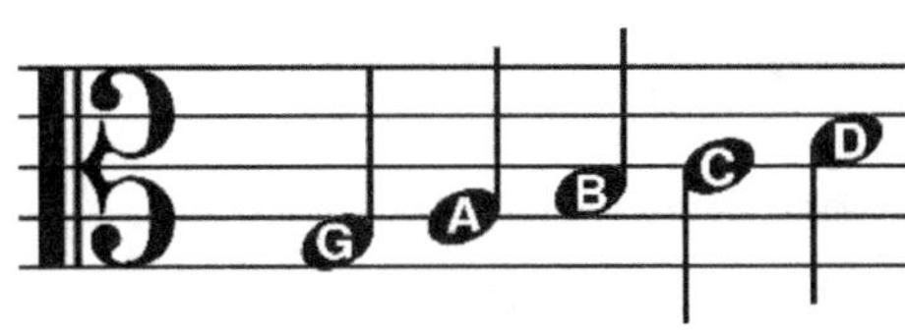

In this part of the book, we will use the G-A-B-C-D notes. Write a song by adding one more Quarter Note in each measure below. When you're done try playing your song to see how it sounds! To finish, title your song!

TITLE: ____

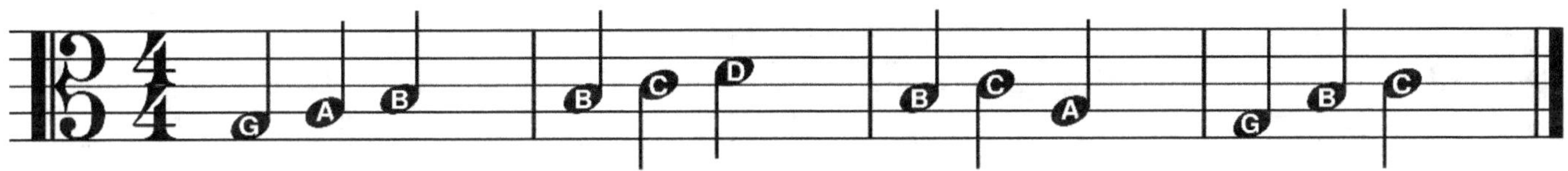

TITLE: <u>CLIMBING THE MOUNTAIN</u>

Climbing mountains can be some hard, but fun work! Finish each measure to write your Climbing Song by drawing two more quarter notes to each measure using the notes G-A-B-C-D.

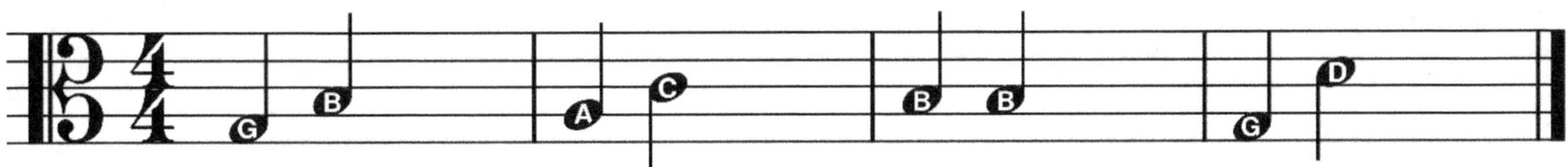

TITLE: <u>GENTLE RAINFALL</u>

You look up at the sky and see the clouds roll in and raindrops start falling. How does this make you feel or think? Complete each measure by writing two more quarter notes in each measure using G-A-B-C-D notes.

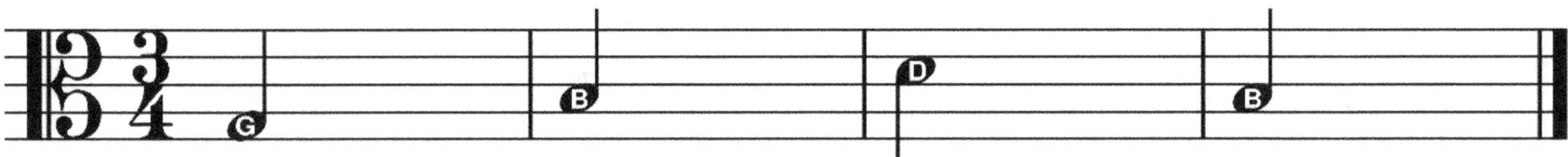

TITLE: <u>THE VIDEO GAME</u>

You've had a long day and you can't wait to sit down and play your favorite video game. Think of that as you fill in the two blank measures with four quarter notes using G-A-B-C-D.

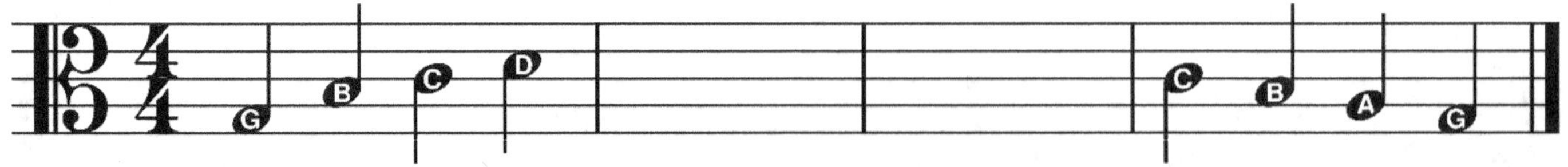

You're not an early riser and today you woke up at noon! Using the notes G-A-B-C-D write out a song about waking up in the afternoon. Each measure should have four quarter notes in it. Once you are done writing, title the song!

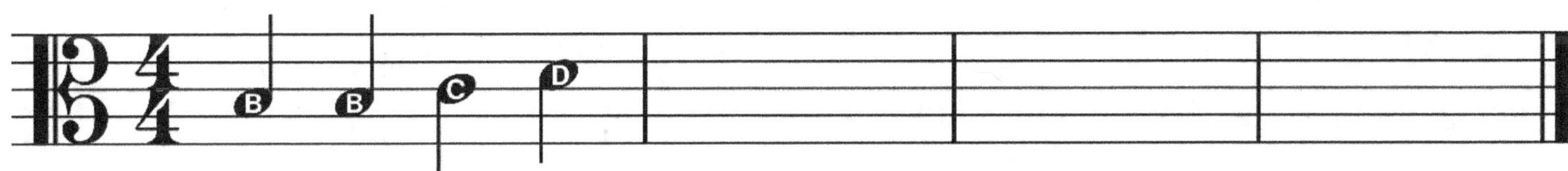

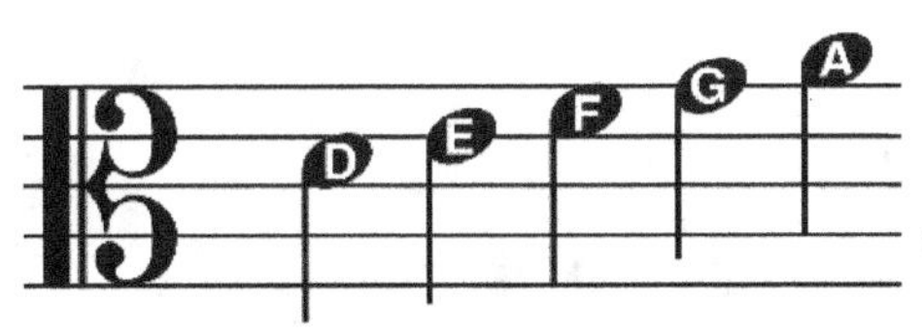

In this part of the book, we will use the D-E-F-G-A notes. Write a song by adding one more Quarter Note in each measure below. When you're done try playing your song to see how it sounds! To finish, title your song!

TITLE: ____

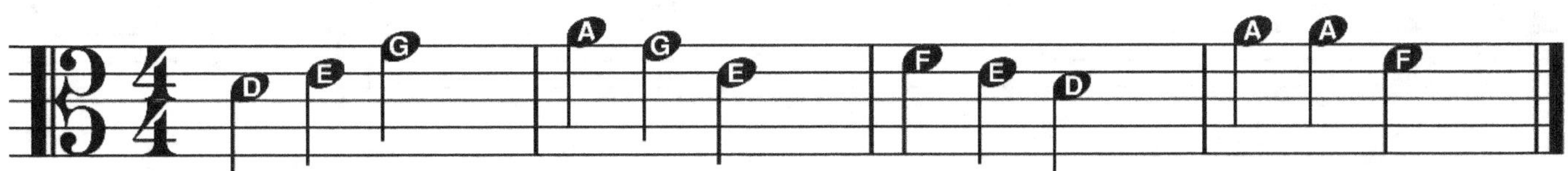

TITLE: ____

Come up with another song using the notes D-E-F-G-A, and give each measure two more quarter notes. Also, give your song a title!

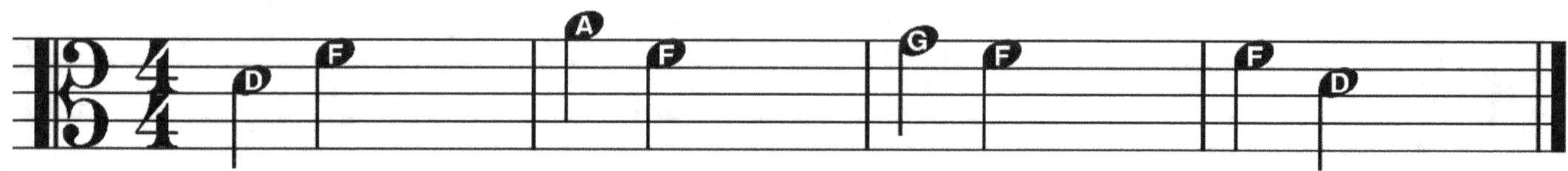

TITLE: <u>THE GROSS DINNER</u>

Have you ever eaten a dinner that was completely gross? Give each measure three more quarter notes using the notes D-E-F-G-A.

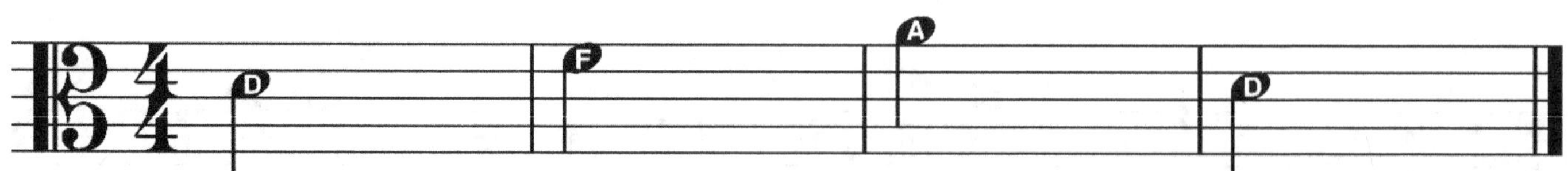

In this song, use the notes D-E-F-G-A and fill in the blank measures with four quarter notes. Once complete, give your song a title!

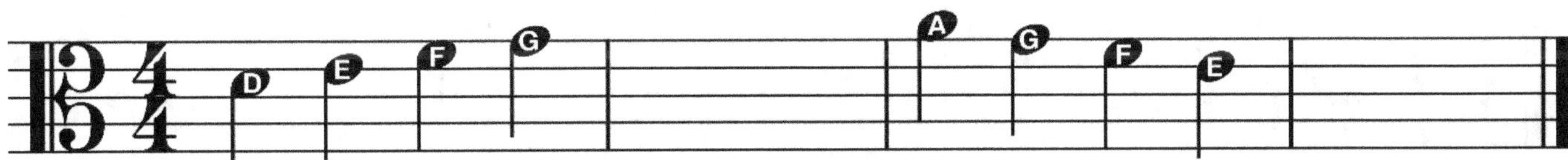

TITLE: <u>THE NIGHT LIGHT</u>

Sometimes, a light on when we sleep is comforting to keep the monsters away. Write a song with D-E-F-G-A about sounds that may frighten you at night. Remember that each measures needs four quarter notes!

TITLE: _______________________________

Think of a time when you had to to take a long car ride. Using the notes of
C-D-E-F-G, come up with a "bored" song. Each measure needs four quarter notes
in it. Don't forget to title the song, too!

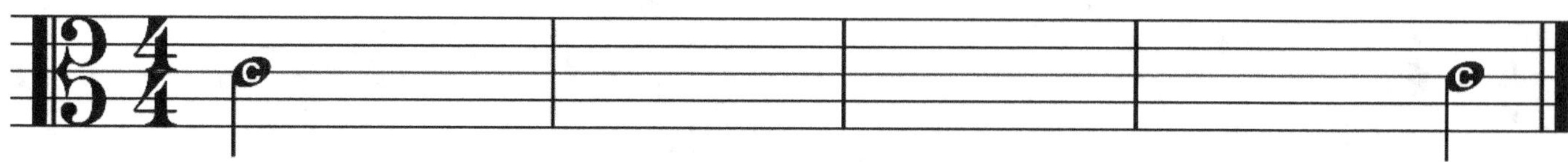

TITLE: <u>KNOCK THREE TIMES</u>

Complete the song below by using the C-D-E-F-G notes. Each measure should
have three quarter notes in it.

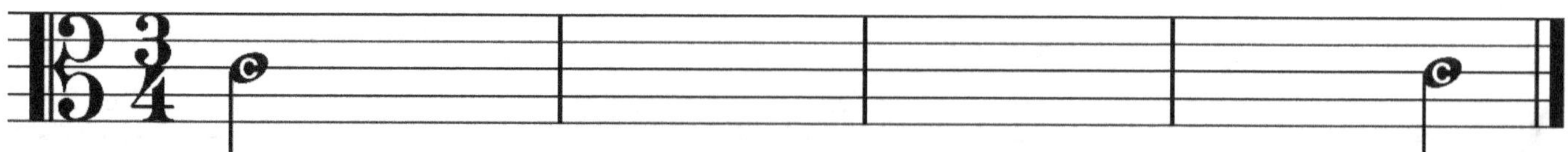

TITLE: <u>C TO MIDDLE C</u>

Using the notes of C-D-E-F-G, write out your song in the measures below. EAch measure should have four quarter notes in it.

TITLE: <u>COMBO NUMBER THREE</u>

Using any note you have learned in the song, fill each measure with three quarter notes to write your song.

On this song, fill in the measures with any note you've learned in this book and title your song!

TITLE: ____

On this song, fill in the measures with any note you learned in this book and title your song!

TITLE: ____

On this song, fill in the measures with any note you've learned in this book and title your song!

TITLE: ____

For your last song, fill in the measures with any note you learned in this book and title your song!

TITLE: ____

EXTRA PAGES FOR
MORE SONGS!

Hey Composer! The next few pages includes staffs that are blank so you can write more songs if you've already filled up this entire book!
Happy Composing!

On this song, fill in the measures with any note you've learned in this book and title your song!

TITLE: ____

On this song, fill in the measures with any note you learned in this book and title your song!

TITLE: ____

On this song, fill in the measures with any note you've learned in this book and title your song!

TITLE: ____

On this song, fill in the measures with any note you learned in this book and title your song!

TITLE: ____

On this song, fill in the measures with any note you've learned in this book and title your song!

TITLE: ____

For your last song, fill in the measures with any note you learned in this book and title your song!

TITLE: ____

On this song, write in a time signature, fill in the measures with any note you've learned in this book and title your song!

TITLE: ____

On this song, write in a time signature,fill in the measures with any note you learned in this book and title your song!

TITLE: ____

On this song, fill in the measures with any note you've learned in this book and title your song!

TITLE: ____

For your last song, fill in the measures with any note you learned in this book and title your song!

TITLE: ____

On this song, fill in the measures with any note you've learned in this book and title your song!

TITLE: ____

On this song, fill in the measures with any note you learned in this book and title your song!

TITLE: ____

On this song, fill in the measures with any note you've learned in this book and title your song!

TITLE: ____

On this song, fill in the measures with any note you learned in this book and title your song!

TITLE: ____

On this song, write in a time signature, fill in the measures with any note you've learned in this book and title your song!

TITLE: ____

On this song, write in a time signature, fill in the measures with any note you learned in this book and title your song!

TITLE: ____

On this song, write in a time signature, fill in the measures with any note you've learned in this book and title your song!

TITLE: ____

On this song, write in a time signature, fill in the measures with any note you learned in this book and title your song!

TITLE: ____